NEGOTIATION
HACKS

NEGOTIATION

EXPERT TACTICS TO GET
WHAT YOU WANT

SIMON RYCRAFT

Published by Hacks Capital, LLC
Austin, TX

www.hackscapital.com

For ordering information or special discounts for bulk purchases,
please contact sales at sales@hackscapital.com.

Design and composition by Kim Lance

Printed in the United States of America on acid-free paper

First Edition

To my parents, who taught me
the importance of empathy, humor, and hard work.

NEGOTIATION HACKS

INTRODUCTION   1

HACK ❶ NON-VERBAL COMMUNICATION   7
The importance of mastering how to recognize and control
non-verbal communication techniques is rarely discussed.

HACK ❷ ARISTOTLE   21
The fundamentals of persuasion date back over 2,300 years.

HACK ❸ STYLES   33
Knowing your own negotiating style, how to read other
people's styles, and adapt accordingly is critical.

HACK ❹ BEHIND THE MASK   45
Personal needs impact even the largest commercial corporate deals.

HACK ❺ THE LAW OF ATTRACTION   59
An expert negotiator maximizes their personal level of magnetism
in order to drive negotiation success.

HACK ❻ GAME PLAN   73
Preparation is key; knowing how and what to prepare requires
focus and attention.

CONCLUSION   87

ACKNOWLEDGMENTS   91

NOTES/REFERENCES/CITATIONS   93

ABOUT THE AUTHOR   97

INTRODUCTION

The official meaning of the term "negotiation" is a formal discussion between two or more people trying to reach an agreement (excluding basic trades and bartering). While the act of negotiating is both an art as well as a science, anyone with the right insights and support can rise to the ranks of an expert negotiator. You don't need to be a practitioner with 30 years of experience or a mind-reader or someone who was just born with significant leverage, nor do you need to be an ex-FBI agent (although that surely can help). You do, however, need to be prepared, whether you have five minutes or five months before your negotiation formally begins.

This book focuses on six distinct and proven hacks that are easy to learn, easy to implement, and accessible to anyone. These hacks have been gathered from my academic pursuits and experiences in working with hundreds of companies, from Silicon Valley and Silicon Hills startups to the Fortune 500. What I have learned is that regardless of the complexity of a negotiation, anyone will benefit from an appreciation of and the deployment of these negotiation hacks. Negotiations

I have personally supported include individual salary negotiations, $100MM+ company contracts, and M&A as well as divestiture activities.

Rather than just rely on my own experiences, I also received and gathered first-hand insights and references from various prominent philosophers, gurus, psychologists, behavioral scientists, and business management experts.

Examples of situations in which these hacks are of most value include:

→ Startup founders who are fundraising or negotiating with large enterprise clients;

→ Corporate development or investment banking teams working on an M&A deal;

→ Sales leaders who must improve their pipeline conversion rate;

→ Purchasing directors negotiating with suppliers;

→ Technology executives finalizing a major outsourcing contract;

→ Trainee attorneys/lawyers looking to sharpen their persuasion skills;

→ And the list goes on . . .

My aim is not to offer a new negotiation framework that is only slightly different from the many that already exist today, but rather to summarize what I believe to be the most important negotiation hacks that you can digest in a few hours and then re-visit at a later date. The real skill comes from testing out the various techniques for yourself and, as always, practice makes perfect.

At the end of each chapter is a quick reference hack summary and two blank pages for notes, if needed.

HACK

1

"The most important thing
in communication is hearing
what isn't said."[1]

–PETER F. DRUCKER

NON-VERBAL COMMUNICATION

W hile verbal and written communications are the focus of most inter-personal exchanges during a negotiation, being aware of and controlling your non-verbal communication is just as important (Hack #1).

The study of this topic can be traced back to the year 1872 in Charles Darwin's book *The Expression of the Emotions in Man and Animal*. Darwin wrote that "the young and the old of widely different races, both with man and animals, express the same state of mind by the same movements."[2]

Following on from Darwin's studies, there has been extensive additional research into non-verbal communication, four key insights of which I find particularly important to understand in the context of a negotiation.

1. BODY LANGUAGE

The "chameleon effect," also known as mimicry, or copying how someone is sitting or standing, is often seen as an approach to signal that two or more people agree with each other and have/or are building a good rapport.[3] Have you ever found yourself subconsciously copying how someone is crossing their arms or legs?

It's important to note that negotiators who are already aware of the benefits of mimicry will often use it strategically, copying your gestures to deliberately try and accelerate the building of a relationship. The next chance you get, have some fun with it. You can easily catch someone else who is consciously aware of this technique by randomly moving your seated position and taking note of how quickly the other person responds in the same way.

"Proxemics" is another key, albeit somewhat more subtle, non-verbal communication consideration. Proxemics focuses on the physical distance between people as they interact. Ever felt incredibly uncomfortable or pressured when a stranger, acquaintance, or co-worker stood a little too close? Did you move away immediately or try and back off slowly, to avoid causing insult? As you can imagine, being too close to another person can completely interrupt a negotiation's progress and flow. It's important for each party to feel that their personal space is being respected. As a guide, in most countries you should sit or stand at least four feet away to avoid causing any discomfort.[4]

One of the main reasons to be mindful of non-verbal communication is that it can give you insights into another person's sincerity. When someone says that they cannot provide a further price discount or they don't have the budget to cover the cost of your services, keep their non-verbal communication in view.

According to Albert Mehrabian (Professor Emeritus of Psychology, UCLA) in his book *Silent Messages, Implicit Communication of Emotions and Attitudes*, deceitful communicators, compared with truthful ones, are thought to:

→ Nod and gesture less;

→ Less frequently move their legs and feet while seated;

→ Lean forward less;

→ Use less eye contact;

→ Talk less, talk more slowly;

→ Use more speech errors;

→ Smile more.

Professor Mehrabian also found that increased physical self-manipulation or adjustments (scratching your head, touching your arm or face) also indicates deceit, presumably associated with the sub-conscious reaction to the general discomfort that some people have when telling a lie.[5]

A critical delivery tip when it comes to non-verbal communication is the need to keep your non-verbal cues, such as body language, in tune with your personal style and what is being said. Remember, the other person will be looking to see if your physical gestures mirror your words; when in doubt, keep them both open and positive. Look out for inconsistencies in how the other negotiating party is sitting in alignment with what they are saying as well as in alignment with the messaging being delivered by other members of their team, if present. A good example here could be if you are crossing your arms and legs but telling the other party you are open for a long term relationship.

2. EYE CONTACT

The connection of eye contact in communication and interpersonal interactions is with us from birth. In a study conducted by neuropsychologists, Sarah Jessen and Tobias Grossman, *"Unconscious Discrimination of Social Cues from Eye Whites in Infants,"* the brains of four-month-olds showed higher levels of activity when they were processing the gazing face of an adult versus an adult that was looking away; at seven months, the infants' brains showed higher levels of activity even when they saw another person's eyes for only 50 milliseconds versus a face with averted eyes—far too quick for any kind of conscious awareness.[6]

To try to identify the optimum length of unbroken eye contact to make another group of psychologists recruited participants at London's Science Museum and asked them to rate how comfortable they found different lengths of eye contact made by faces shown in video clips, ranging from between 100ms (a tenth of a second) to 10,300ms (just over ten seconds). On average, the participants were most comfortable with eye contact that lasted just over three seconds.[7]

While a three-second rule should likely vary in a negotiation when you are listening versus speaking, it is a great guide to help ensure you are sufficiently engaging with the other negotiating party so that every message is delivered with maximum impact. I also highlight how eye contact is important in chapter 5 in reference to the "law of attraction."

I personally struggle with controlling eye contact more than the other controllable non-verbal communication levers. I have been told I don't do it enough, and when I try to improve, I often get some funny looks. The difference between good eye contact and staring is a fine dividing line that one day I hope to master. It is often said that "eyes are the windows of the soul," so it's important to try and get it right. If used correctly, eye contact has the power to instill trust and, as mentioned above, avoid creating the perception of deceit.

3. PARA-LINGUISTICS

Para-linguistics is the study of *how* something is said, not *what* is said. Strong links have been found between arousal cues (facial and vocal activity, speech rate and volume) and the persuasiveness of the accompanying messages. For example, faster-talking individuals are deemed more persuasive, as are speakers who use varied tones to avoid being monotonic.[8] Louder volumes also appear more persuasive; however this is likely limited and does not include volumes that can be interpreted as shouting.

4. HEALTH

Trying to stay healthy, in both body and mind, is something that is rarely linked to negotiating; however, it can play an important part. While our health is not completely under our control, there are some elements of it that can be managed by choice. Eating healthily, exercising regularly, and getting enough sleep are all factors that can impact our performance in a negotiation. As Arianna Huffington (world-famous author and CEO of Thrive Global) states in her book *Thrive: The Third Metric to Redefining Success and Creating a Life of Well-Being, Wisdom, and Wonder*, sleep deprivation, for example, "reduces our emotional intelligence, self-regard, assertiveness, sense of independence, empathy toward others, the quality of our interpersonal relationships, positive thinking, and impulse control."[9]

HACK ❶
SUMMARY

It is critical to be mindful of non-verbal communication techniques (only relevant for in-person or videoconference-based negotiations). Key attributes to look out for and be in control of during your negotiation include:

a. "Body Language"

    i. "Chameleon effect" the technique of either subconsciously or consciously copying another person's body language to signal you agree with them or as an attempt to accelerate a trust-based relationship;

    ii. "Proxemics" the appropriate use of physical distance between you and the other people you are negotiating with to avoid unnecessary discomfort;

b. Eye contact, to support the verbal message being delivered is received clearly and to express that you are fully engaged in the conversation;

c. "Para-linguistics", which includes talking faster with varied tones and louder volumes, can help improve your perceived persuasiveness. However, it is important to note that these should all be applied within reason. Talking too fast, too varied and too loud can be viewed as confusing, rude and disruptive;

d. Good health, where it can be controlled, can help you increase factors such as emotional intelligence and empathy to help drive better negotiation results.

WHITE SPACE FOR NOTES

WHITE SPACE FOR NOTES

HACK

②

"But when you read back verbatim

What they're saying to persuade them

They realize exactly how I've played them."[10]

—DAN THE AUTOMATOR & PRINCE PAUL

ARISTOTLE

Negotiations are often seen as a battle where each person must use their skills to defeat the other opponent(s), tricking them into submission. The reality is generally less dramatic, where each person's goal is to get a better deal than the one originally on the table. While many negotiation books and training materials reference hostage situations, I prefer to focus on the techniques that will help drive success in more likely business scenarios.

In any given negotiation there are a few core, overarching persuasion techniques which, I argue, are just as relevant now as they were 2,300 years ago.

The king of persuasion, Aristotle (who lived 384–322 BCE), is commonly considered one of the fathers of philosophy. His work encompassed research in biology, astronomy, geology, physics, psychology, economics and poetry. In his second book, *Rhetoric*, he outlined three core principles of persuasion that any speaker needs to display to convince their audience to believe their story or argument.[11] Hack #2 is learning how to apply these same three principles in any negotiation you are conducting.

Ethos, the first principle of persuasion, is the relation that an audience has with the character of the speaker. By character, Aristotle was referring to trust. To persuade someone to follow you and either meet, or get closer to, your negotiation demands and goals, you must first gain their trust.

Trust is much easier to build over time through experiences in interacting with another person or company than it is to develop in a short period. This is especially true if the person you are working with has never met you before. In many situations you will likely start at a disadvantage due to certain factors that might seem outside of your control. These factors can include any or all the following:

→ The individual you are negotiating with
   is naturally mistrusting of others;

→ The company you work for has been shown
   to be untrustworthy in the past in working with
   this individual or business;

→ You already did or said something during
   the negotiation that has put your credibility
   into question by mistake.

KEY TIPS TO BUILDING UP
YOUR PERCEIVED TRUSTWORTHINESS

1. **Spotlight connections:** Make your connections visible to other individuals or groups that you know are trusted by and familiar to the other negotiating party. Beyond making your connections clear, it is always worth getting a proactive reference, such as asking one or more of your connections to reach out to the other negotiating party in advance. Another more subtle alternative is to mention a recent meeting or phone conversation with that trusted connection. Be wary of saying things such as, "Oh, by the way, I went to high school with your CIO." If you haven't spoken to that CIO/person for over 20 years and are purely name dropping, it can have the opposite of the desired effect.

2. **Everyone loves a storyteller:** Tell stories about yourself and your company. Try to ensure it is clear how your or your company's mission is directly aligned with your negotiation goals. This technique is used by some of the most successful startup founders I know who use storytelling to fundraise and secure investments that would otherwise never be possible from traditional sources such as a bank loan. Paul J. Zak (Founding Director of the

Center for Neuroeconomics Studies and a professor of economics, psychology, and management at Claremont Graduate University) studied this technique in his book, *Trust Factor: The Science of Creating High-Performance Companies.* In the early 1990s, Professor Zak's lab discovered that a neurochemical called oxytocin is produced by the brain to signal, "it's safe to approach others."[12] Oxytocin motivates cooperation with others. It does this by enhancing the sense of empathy, our ability to experience others' emotions. After running multiple studies, Professor Zak's team found that the use of character-driven storytelling is a key trigger for oxytocin synthesis.

It is also worth noting that the type of story being told is important. According to a study by Professors Daniel T. Gilbert and Gus Cooney (Department of Psychology, Harvard University) and Timothy D. Wilson (University of Virginia) listeners enjoy hearing familiar stories much more than novel ones, so ensure your stories are as relevant and succinct as possible.[13]

3. **Credential but don't brag:** Present your credentials to the other negotiating party. This can be simply done by ensuring to include your title in an email (you might be surprised how many people don't do this) or reaching out to the person(s) by sending them a LinkedIn

invite. There is also no harm in referencing your credentials while telling a story, but don't overdo it and avoid repeating yourself or bragging. No one likes a showoff.

4. **Earn it:** Review ways in which you can show that you are trustworthy. When a company doesn't have a long list of credentials or, for example, weak financials (the case for many startups/younger companies), the trust that the CEO, founders, or senior team can instill with potential investors becomes super critical. Trust signals, such as hitting previously forecasted revenue or new customer acquisition targets, can all go a long way.

Pathos, the second principle of persuasion, is the concern that you need to have with the emotions of the other negotiating party. Humans are emotional beings, despite our desire to think we are rational decision makers. With this in mind, it is important to identify ways to arouse the emotions of the person(s) you are negotiating with. Give the other negotiating party evidence of how easy it is to do business with you. Simple gestures that can help include, for example, arranging the logistics for your next meeting, opening doors for people at their office, or remembering to say "please" and "thank you." If the other party sees that working with you is more like a meaningful long-term relationship rather than a one-off transaction, they will want to support your goals. These approaches might seem obvious but should not be over looked. We will also cover this as a stand-alone hack in chapter 5, on the Law of Attraction.

The third and final principle of persuasion is **Logos,** the reasonableness of your argument.

While being both trusted and empathetic to the other negotiating party is important, you will also need to provide hard facts, references, and research to back up your claims.

Logos can be as simple as providing statistics that the other party may not know or quoting specific facts: for example, "80% of our customers renew their subscriptions every year" or "on average our clients double their net operating income within the first six months of using our services."

As noted by the late Dr. James C. McCroskey (a renowned expert in communication studies), "Including good evidence may significantly increase immediate audience attitude and source credibility." Dr. McCroskey also found that the use of evidence and logic is less important or effective if you are already well known by the audience.[14] Irrespective of how you intend to use the power of Logos, always be prepared to provide back-up evidence and/or use a third-party firm to help validate your arguments.

HACK ❷ SUMMARY

a. Applying Aristotle's three key principles of persuasion can help you improve your negotiation position.

b. Each principle is less effective if used without the other two.

c. The first principle, **Ethos**, deals with the need to ensure that the other negotiating party trusts you. Key tips to doing this include:

    i. Make visible your connections to other people that they trust and/or respect;

    ii. Use storytelling as a more persuasive way to explain your background and why you need certain things during the negotiation;

    iii. Make clear your credentials;

    iv. Practice what you preach.

d. The second principle, **Pathos**, guides us on the importance of appreciating the emotions of the other negotiating party. To evoke positive emotions, show the other party how easy you are to do business with; make them feel comfortable and at ease.

e. The final principle, **Logos**, highlights the importance of using logic as part of your negotiation. For example, conduct and share the results of market research or price benchmarking to back up your claims.

WHITE SPACE FOR NOTES

WHITE SPACE FOR NOTES

HACK
3

"There are times when I am so unlike myself that I might be taken for someone else of an entirely opposite character."[15]

—JEAN-JACQUES ROUSSEAU

STYLES

ack #3 is the need to understand your own personal negotiating style as well as the necessity to adapt your style depending on whom you are negotiating with.

Your negotiating style, while mostly sub-conscious, includes various elements and preferences such as where the negotiation is located (your office, their office, or neutral ground; in-person vs. remote), the team structure you like to use, and your go-to list of tactics (more about these in Hack #6). To better understand your own negotiating style, look no further than your personality type. Extroverts, for example, are known to display certain personality traits, which can include wanting to be the center of attention and/or regularly talking about their own feelings and emotions out loud. In a negotiation setting, these personalities will want to define the negotiation agenda, will try to control the flow of information and communication, and will make demands early and more frequently than other personality types.

Before we delve into the multiple dimensions of negotiating styles it is helpful to take a step back to look at where the study into various personality types is commonly believed to have begun.

In order to do this, we again need to turn to another well-known Greek philosopher, Hippocrates (460–370 BCE). Hippocrates is considered the father of modern medicine, also credited with his research into the study of the Four Temperaments theory. The theory suggests there are four fundamental personality types: **sanguine, choleric, melancholic,** and **phlegmatic**. Hippocrates described the four temperaments as part of the ancient medical concept of humorism, linking four specific bodily fluids to everyone's personality traits and behaviors. While the last 2,000 years has cast doubt on the correlation between bodily fluids and types, the underlying psychological principles that Hippocrates devised still apply today.[16] Even though most people are a blend of these four personality types, we all have certain personality traits that play a more dominant role in how we interact with others.[17]

→ People with a **Choleric** personality are said to be passionate, ambitious, and bold;

→ People with a **Melancholic** personality are predominantly reserved, anxious, and unhappy;

→ People with a **Sanguine** personality are joyful, eager, and optimistic;

→ People who have a **Phlegmatic** personality are said to be calm, reliable, and thoughtful.

More recent research has taken the four basic personality types and styles and developed a much larger and more complex series of variations. Researchers famed for developing new frameworks in this academic arena include Carl Jung ("Jungian Typology"),[18] William Marston, interestingly the same guy who invented the first lie detector test and created the comic book hero Wonder Woman, (his book is titled *Emotions of Normal People*),[19] David Keirsey (author of *Please Understand Me*),[20] Isabel Briggs Myers and Katharine Cooks Myers (creators of the Myers-Briggs Type Indicators),[21] and David Kolb (developer of Experiential Learning Theory).[22] What the collective work of these psychologists helps to reinforce is that our personality and style are driven by a mixture of our unique genetics and life experiences. In summary, no person is the same.

But what does this all mean in helping you to best optimize your performance in a negotiation?

1. First understand your own personality style by taking

one of the various tests available online, such as MBTI (https://www.mbtionline.com) or Keirsey (https://www. keirsey.com). Alternatively, give two or three of your friends the list of four personality types, with a brief description of the related key traits, and ask them to summarize which type best describes you.

2. Observe the four personality types in your friends and/ or work colleagues and look for patterns in how they act. Are they displaying one personality type all the time or switching styles in different settings (such as a large group meeting versus a one-on-one discussion)?

3. Appreciate how different personality types have differing needs. How do you persuade/negotiate with someone who displays signs of the **Choleric** personality versus someone who displays signals of **Phlegmatic?** People who use the same negotiating style all the time, regardless of who they are negotiating with, will struggle to consistently hit their negotiation targets/goals.

4. The fun comes with learning how to adapt your own style to suit the situation. If you are someone who leans towards displays of the **Choleric** personality during a negotiation, you will find it much harder to instill Ethos/Trust

in a new acquaintance if that person has a mainly **Melancholic** personality. You can still be authentic in your negotiations, but using techniques akin to the **Phlegmatic** personality will generally be more effective in getting what you want.

While adapting your style to suit the situation may make a lot of sense, it isn't necessarily that easy. Professor Albert Mehrabian, referenced in chapter 1, is also well known for his research into people's social styles. Professor Mehrabian highlights that "people are generally able to control only very superficial aspects of their behavior and self-presentation" (such as what they are wearing, personal grooming, and how they might phrase sentences). The fundamental aspects of an individual's personality type are much more difficult to alter and won't be easy to change overnight. This aligns directly with Austrian neurologist Sigmund Freud's work on the psychodynamic theory of the human psyche, which first popularized the concept of the subconscious and how it controls our everyday actions. Being able to adapt your personality type and subsequent negotiation style in a somewhat agile and reactive way, especially under pressure or stress, is a skill that takes focus, discipline, and lots of coaching and practice.

HACK ❸ SUMMARY

a. Negotiating styles are typically linked to a person's personality type. Taking the lead from Hippocrates, there are four basic personality types:

   i. People with a Choleric personality are said to be passionate, ambitious, and bold;

   ii. People with a Melancholic personality are predominantly reserved, anxious, and unhappy;

   iii. People with a Sanguine personality are joyful, eager, and optimistic;

   iv. People who have a Phlegmatic personality are said to be calm, reliable, and thoughtful.

b. To understand your own style, take one of the various tests available online such as https://www.mbtionline.com/ or https://www.keirsey.com/, or ask a few close friends and colleagues for their opinion and compare the results.

c. Be mindful of how your dominant negotiating style may potentially conflict with the other negotiating party and adapt accordingly.

d. While adapting your style to suit the negotiation may make a lot of sense, it isn't necessarily that easy. Practice makes perfect.

WHITE SPACE FOR NOTES

WHITE SPACE FOR NOTES

HACK

4

"You will get all you want

in life if you help enough other people

get what they want."[23]

—ZIG ZIGLAR

BEHIND THE MASK

B ehind every comment, facial expression, and body movement is a complex web of perspectives, bias, interests, and desires. Finding out as much as you can about the other negotiating parties' needs and wants (Hack #4) gets you closer to appreciating their position and strategizing how you can use that understanding to your advantage.

In order to truly appreciate another person's desires, you first need to learn more about them. The three key sources you can use to help reduce information asymmetries include:

1. Online research about individuals (details typically found on websites such as LinkedIn as well as from a basic Google or Bing search)

THE WHAT	THE WHY
A. **REVIEW HOW LONG THEY HAVE BEEN AT THEIR CURRENT COMPANY AND IN THEIR CURRENT ROLE. ALSO CHECK WHERE THEY HAVE WORKED IN THE PAST. SEE IF THEY HAVE SHIFTED ROLES AND PROFESSIONS MULTIPLE TIMES OR DONE THE SAME WORK IN THE SAME OR A SIMILAR INDUSTRY FOR MOST OF THEIR CAREER.**	**i.** These insights help you determine how experienced the individual may be. If they have worked as an aerospace engineer for 30 years, it's very likely they will know more about the industry than you do, so trying to persuade them that your new product is better than anyone else's on the market today won't be easy.
	ii. If they are new to their role, be mindful they are looking to prove themselves and will be cautious of trusting a new individual that they or their company has never interacted with before.
	iii. If they have been in the same role at the same company for between 3 and 5 years, unless they are close to retirement, it's possible they are looking for a promotion so will be eager to deliver or be involved in a project or new venture that supports, rather than hinders, that goal.

THE WHAT	THE WHY
B. **CHECK THE COMPANIES AND ASSOCIATIONS THEY FOLLOW OR ARE AFFILIATED WITH.**	**i.** If they are connected to certain professional or industry associations, this can highlight the depth at which they are psychologically and emotional tied to their job. If you can help them win an award that is recognized by their industry peers or connect them with someone well respected in the same industry eco-system, then you are providing them with much more value than they may get elsewhere.
	ii. If they are connected to a charity/non-profit or sports association, that can indicate a non-work-related topic you might have in common. Awareness of the interests they have outside of work can be used to highlight to them that you are interested in them as a person and not in just this negotiation.
C. **TAKE NOTE OF ANY MUTUAL CONNECTIONS YOU MIGHT HAVE.**	**i.** Identifying mutual connections can give you insights into the person themselves. People typically connect with those of like minds. As mentioned in chapter 2, this can help you build trust if any of the mutual connections are strong and are willing to act as your reference.

2. Online research about the company (again from basic Google searches looking for recent company news, history of the company culture, how/when the company was founded, and a look at their published financial statements, if available)

THE WHAT	THE WHY
A. NEWS FOUND ONLINE CAN RANGE FROM RECENT ANNOUNCEMENTS SUCH AS M&A ACTIVITY TO PUBLIC RELATIONS UPDATES (BOTH POSITIVE AND NEGATIVE).	**i.** Reading recent news gives you insights into hot topics that the individual and their company may be facing. You can use it purely to show you care about the company, to pay a compliment (for example, "congratulations on the recent acquisition of x"), or, if you are lucky, your product and/or service may be of value in an issue that the company is currently facing. Maybe they just had a customer data security breach, and your company provides PR services on demand to help with those exact types of situations.

THE WHAT	THE WHY
B. A REVIEW OF FINANCIAL STATEMENTS, SUCH AS 10-KS, 10-QS, 8-KS, S-1S, AND S-4S PROVIDES LOTS OF DATA POINTS AROUND THE COMPANY'S RECENT ACTIVITY AND FINANCIAL HEALTH AS WELL AS INSIGHTS INTO THE PERFORMANCE OF VARIOUS PRODUCTS, BUSINESS DIVISIONS, AND/OR REGIONS.	**i.** If you are not a financial analyst or well versed on how to interpret various financial statements, you can always ask someone in your finance department for their opinion. Alternatively, you can review summary material found on websites such as Yahoo! Finance, Google Finance, Motley Fool, MSN Money, or Morningstar. **ii.** In doing your research, look for recent financial quarter announcements and trends in financial metrics that you may be able to help influence, such as net income or gross revenues.

3. Offline research

THE WHAT	THE WHY
A. REACH OUT TO CATCH UP WITH ANY MUTUAL CONNECTIONS YOU MIGHT HAVE, BUT ONLY IF YOU TRULY TRUST THAT CONNECTION.	**i.** In addition to just name-dropping your mutual connections and using them as a reference for your credibility, you may also want to talk to them "offline" and ask for any tips they can provide on working with the individual and/or company that you are negotiating with. They may hold insightful content on the culture of the company or how to navigate around negotiation obstacles.
B. ASK THE PERSON YOU ARE NEGOTIATING WITH SOME DIRECT QUESTIONS. THIS IS A GOOD WAY TO TEST OUT THE OTHER RESEARCH YOU HAVE DONE AND ALSO TO DOUBLE-CHECK YOUR ASSUMPTIONS BEFORE RELYING ON THEM TO GUIDE YOUR NEGOTIATION STRATEGY.	**i.** If you cannot find any information of use online then revert to the technique of asking questions. It is amazing how much you can find out about someone during a negotiation just by asking. You will learn things about them that even their close friends or colleagues didn't know. This approach is also known as the Socratic Method, so named after another Greek philosopher, Socrates.

THE WHAT	THE WHY
B. (CONTINUED)	**ii.** When I work with corporate executives in a training room environment, I often play a fake magic trick with someone from the audience. While the person selected may seem random, as with most magic tricks, the person is always picked on purpose. I ask them to write the answers to three questions on a piece of paper and hand it to someone else in the room. I pretend to harness mind-reading powers and begin to write down the answers on a whiteboard in the room. Nine out of ten times the person selected and most of the people in the room are shocked by the game. The secret is purely from doing some online research about that individual before the training session started. One thing that never ceases to amaze me is how many people in the room are unaware of the answers to the questions despite sometimes having worked with that person for several years. The questions are generally straightforward, such as which city you went to college in, what month were you born, or what is your favorite color. Having one question such as their favorite color {which I often get wrong, as this is rarely searchable online}. Hack #5 will go into more depth on the importance of using questions and active listening to gain trust and improve your likeability. What the magic trick highlights is that by asking only a few basic questions you are already at a competitive advantage over the other people that they may be negotiating with.

To truly understand another person's needs and wants it takes much more than pure research. It requires you to empathize with the other negotiating party. Putting yourself in their shoes (the individual, team and/or company) allows you to appreciate why the negotiation even started in the first place and the direction that it needs to take in order for you to be successful. If you do your research but don't put it to use with empathy, then the negotiation will either take longer than necessary, or hit a deadlock, or end with no apparent option for revival.

In an interview with Sam Richards (senior lecturer in sociology at Pennsylvania State University), I asked, "How does empathy empower?" Sam responded with, "True power comes from understanding; true understanding cannot occur unless we allow ourselves to be vulnerable enough to say, 'I don't know that person's story and I really do want to know.' That's the foundation of true empathy and it requires open and vulnerable communication." According to Sam, many people attempt to be empathetic but fall short and are merely tolerating or sympathizing at best, both of which are significantly less effective.

While being empathetic to the other person can help with your negotiation, it is important to avoid misuse. If you are not careful with the information you have found, especially personal information, it can raise a red flag that you might be untrustworthy and have the opposite to the desired effect. Your research can also drive you to make incorrect assumptions: for example, assuming someone of British descent is a tea-drinking soccer fan, or that all Japanese people like sushi and karaoke.

In addition to empathizing with another person or company's goals, make sure you underscore how your goals align with theirs. The rule of reciprocity (made popular by Robert Cialdini, professor emeritus of psychology and marketing at Arizona State University and author of *Influence: The Psychology of Persuasion*) is a well-known human condition where people are inherently wired to want to give something back for something received.[24] If they know your goals are aligned with theirs, this can take the power of reciprocity to another level, as they will be more likely to want to achieve those goals together.

HACK ❹
SUMMARY

a. Every person has hidden needs that, if understood, can better help you get what you want during a negotiation.

b. In order to have a better appreciation for the person or company you are negotiating with, do as much online and offline research as possible.

c. Use the research conducted to empathize with the other negotiating party, highlighting clearly how both of your goals are aligned.

d. Avoid using the research to draw any potentially inaccurate conclusions/assumptions. Incorrect assumptions can have the opposite to the desired effect, causing irritation instead of motivation.

WHITE SPACE FOR NOTES

WHITE SPACE FOR NOTES

HACK

5

"If you want to
gather honey, don't kick over
the beehive."[25]

–DALE CARNEGIE

THE LAW OF ATTRACTION

Hack #5 is based on the law of attraction and likeability: its use, misuse, and interpretation. Have you ever consciously noticed there are people who always seem to be more likeable, both during your first interaction with them as well as throughout your personal engagement? Irrespective of your religious, spiritual, or cultural beliefs and values it is hard to deny that you enjoy doing business with some people more than others. Whatever the source of this attraction—be it trust, familiarity, desire, or just how a person makes you feel—understanding this law and the magnetism it can create is a critical step in the path to negotiation enlightenment.

This hack is just as much about realizing how someone's likeability can weaken your negotiating position (unless you stay neutral and resist their magnetism) as it is about learning how you can increase your own appeal.

In order to truly deploy Hack #5, there are six specific techniques that can increase your chance of being liked.

Continuity of use and consistency are also very critical, especially if you will be interacting with the same person multiple times. Without continuity you are in danger of coming across as insincere.

ASK LOTS OF QUESTIONS AND ACTIVELY LISTEN

As noted in Hack #4, asking specific questions can help you understand the other negotiating party's needs beyond your initial assumptions. Another positive effect of using questions, if they are relevant and credible, is that it can increase your likeability.

Actively listening to the person or group you are negotiating with shows them you care about what they are saying, are engaged in the discussion, and have a vested interest in reaching a negotiation solution. The neuroscience behind why people enjoy the attention of being listened to is compelling. A study led by Professor Diana Tamir (Department of Psychology, Princeton University) found that "individuals place high subjective value on opportunities to communicate their thoughts and feelings to others and that doing so engages neural and cognitive mechanisms associated with reward."[26]

Active listening goes beyond just staying silent, though. Everyone, including me, is guilty of either purposefully ignoring what is being said, daydreaming, or just pretending to listen while distracted by other stimuli (like a cell/mobile phone) during a conversation.

TO LISTEN ACTIVELY, FOLLOW THESE 5 SIMPLE RULES:

1. *Concentrate* by mentally absorbing the content in an email or what is being said during a negotiation. These can also include responding to some of the non-verbal cues detailed in Hack #1. If someone appears uncomfortable, offer them a cushion.

2. *Acknowledge* what has been said with facial expressions, changes in body positioning, responding to emails, or by saying a simple "understood" or "ok."

3. Take *full responsibility for the completeness of a message*. If you acknowledge what someone has communicated to you but they later find out you weren't listening, it can have the opposite of the desired effect. Something as simple as verifying the spelling of someone's name when you first meet or asking them to repeat a phrase or comment that you know is important to them or to their negotiation can show you care.

4. Keep *appropriate eye contact* (as also mentioned in Hack #1).

5. *Avoid distractions* when possible. Unintentionally delaying responding to someone's email or staring at your cell phone during a meeting can be important tactics in some settings, but when you are trying to build rapport with another person, these techniques can be perceived as disrespectful.

SELL THE BENEFITS OF THE DEAL

Focusing on the positives and exploring adjustments to the existing deal rather than proposing vastly different alternatives will help to make you and your offer more attractive. Negotiating is foremost a sales activity. You are tasked with selling a solution to the other party. Even if you are the one buying something, you must appreciate the need to sell your terms in order to reach a final agreement.

BE CALMLY CONFIDENT, FRIENDLY, AND POSITIVE

There is unfortunately a very thin line between confidence and arrogance. In fact, ego is often at the center of many nEGOtiations. If you act confident without displaying traces of egotistical behavior, you will be perceived as likeable. If your negotiation opponent enjoys interacting with you, they are more likely to want to reach a negotiation agreement that achieves some or all your goals instead of playing a zero-sum game.

Equal to being confident is the importance of being friendly. This is a key tactic that Tim Sanders (*New York Times* bestselling author, public speaker, and former Yahoo! executive) praises in his book *The Likeability Factor.*[27] Proactively working on being more friendly means:

→ Ensuring everyone you meet feels welcome,

→ Using friendly language, particularly the first name of the person you are talking to,

→ Smiling.

Last but not least is the need to be positive. As Professor Elaine Hatfield (University of Hawaii), Professor John T. Cacioppo (University of Chicago) and Professor Richard Rapson (University of Hawaii) explain in their book *Emotional Contagion*, being positive not only increases your likeability but is also contagious.[28] In a negotiation setting this can have the impact of changing the mood of the other negotiating party. If the other person feels more positive when they are around you, they will be more reasonable and flexible when it comes to trying to accommodate your needs.

GIVE AND TAKE

A no-strings-attached approach to helping others can also make you more likable. As world-famous author Adam Grant writes in his book *Give and Take: A Revolutionary Approach to Success*, "people are attracted to those who care about them."[29]

What is often difficult to assess, though, is someone's true intentions. Giving, especially in a negotiation, can often have hidden and ulterior motives. The best way to give during a negotiation is to focus on providing knowledge or meaningful connections that the other negotiating party values (as previously mentioned in Hack #4).

In addition, it can also help for the other negotiating party to know that you are a giving person in general. This can be evident via references/testimonials or by their learning you are connected to an unrelated third party such as a charity. While this approach is of less use during a one-off single negotiation or if you are negotiating with someone who is extremely self-centered, it can have a positive compound impact if you need to negotiate with that same people/organization again or with someone in their network.

AVOID STRESS/IRRITATORS

Avoiding stress in a negotiation helps to showcase that doing business with you will be a stress-free process. Avoiding stress means avoiding the temptation to use irritators. Potentially offensive comments or gestures often go unnoticed to the person delivering them but can cause discomfort to the receiving party. Irritators can be as subtle as not opening the door for someone or as obvious as the overuse of profanity without justification. Of course, everyone gets irritated in different ways, so if you want to play it safe, just be polite and show respect.

ADMIT YOUR WEAKNESSES

Humility is critical to creating and sustaining attraction. Admitting or displaying your weaknesses is one way to express humility and make yourself more likeable.[30] The best approach to doing this in a corporate setting is to open a meeting by listing the challenges that you are facing upfront, such as, "the reason we are here today is to find a solution to the fact that we need to find an alternative source of supply, as our current provider is too expensive. If we do not find a cheaper option, then we may have no choice but to make headcount reductions." It can also be more subtle and include, for example, admitting your weakness at a sport or in remembering dates or names.

Last, but not least, being liked should not be confused with agreeableness. Acknowledging the other negotiating party's arguments and needs will not weaken your position, if you maintain your ground and don't lose sight of your goals.

HACK ⑤ SUMMARY

a. The law of attraction, if used appropriately, provides you with significant leverage in a negotiation. Not only does it make doing business with you seem more enjoyable for the other negotiating party, it also increases the chances that you will hit your negotiation goals faster.

b. Tactics for using the law of attraction in your favor:

    i. Ask lots of questions and actively listen;

    ii. Work to sell the benefits of the deal to the other party;

    iii. Be calmly confident, friendly, and positive;

    iv. Find ways to give, not just take;

    v. Avoid stress/irritators;

    vi. Admit your weaknesses.

WHITE SPACE FOR NOTES

WHITE SPACE FOR NOTES

HACK

"Victorious warriors win first
and then go to war, while
defeated warriors go to war first
and then seek to win."[31]

—SUN TZU

GAME PLAN

f you have ever taken a formal negotiation training session or seminar, one of the foundational learnings from those investments is the importance of preparation. Hack #6 might seem somewhat counter-intuitive, but expert negotiators will always do more preparation than anyone else, limited only by access to resources and/or the amount of time they have before a negotiation formally begins. When delivering these types of trainings or talks, I focus on the topic of preparation in as short a period as possible, then run mini-case study sessions, allowing the attendees to make use of templates and, most importantly, learn by doing.

While the use of certain tactics during a negotiation may come as second nature, you will find that additional leverage is gained by planning which tactics you intend to use, who should use them, and when.

It may seem that you are always rushing and don't have time to fully prepare. When this happens, ask yourself: Why did I leave it so late? The reality is that negotiations don't begin the first time you meet with the other negotiating party.

Negotiations sometimes begin the first time you communicate with the other party over the phone or over email. During that first interaction they are already marking their position, formulating a view on your style, and pressure testing your weaknesses and potential flaws. Preparation is not just about getting ready for the first in-person meeting; it also applies to the importance of how you conduct business in general (see Hacks #2 and #5).

When you do have enough time to prepare, below is a list of my eight favorite negotiation tactics. As you will notice, the most well-known tactic, called "Good cop, bad cop," has been left out from the list, as I am willing to bet anyone with young kids has to deploy that technique at least three to four times a week.

TACTIC #1: SET THE STRATEGY & ANCHOR

Crafting the parameters within which you can and will negotiate is extremely important. A pre-defined negotiation strategy, for example, allows you to gain alignment from your other negotiation team members but also becomes your cheat sheet to ensure you stay focused, and on track and don't lose control. In its simplest form a negotiation strategy means asking yourself, "What is the lowest point

I can go to, either on price or with a specific contract term, and what is the maximum?"

Have you ever set a budget for buying something, then ended up going outside that range, likely driven by emotion? Have you ever tried to sell something, had a buyer say that your lowest price is too expensive, and walk away without a sale?

I like to picture the negotiation strategy like a sumo wrestling ring, where each person will constantly try to push the other person outside of the ring, purely to test the limits. With a negotiation, once your negotiating strategy has been set, if the other party pushes you outside that ring and refuses to let you back in, you have no choice but to signal a deadlock and walk away.

Having a strategy is great, but you cannot keep it to yourself. Sharing key targets with the other negotiating party, by anchoring your position, will help them determine the range within which they can operate. Don't forget to be both honest and realistic. If for example you say, "The most I could ever pay for this solution is $250K" but then the negotiation ends with you paying $400K, you have immediately lost some credibility if you ever need to negotiate with that same person or company again. Anchoring is when you set a limit in the mind of the other negotiating party to indicate your limitations and goals, i.e. "this is where the boat stops so please don't try and maneuver outside of this zone."

How and when this tactic is used are also critical. In my experience the best approach is to be the first person to drop the anchor and do it as soon as possible. Just like making the first play in any game, it gives you the opportunity to be one step ahead.

TACTIC # 2: TEAMING

Knowing when to negotiate on your own or use a team is a key tactic in itself. Those who enjoy negotiating prefer to dominate the communications and rarely coordinate with others. This can come from a heightened, and potentially inaccurate, belief of self-worth but can also be driven by a lack of experience in negotiating with a team or fear of exposure if, and when, they fail.

On the other side of the spectrum are those people who feel less comfortable negotiating on their own and prefer to delegate the responsibility to someone else whenever possible.

Whatever your position and level of confidence, it is worth reviewing the advantages of teaming in a negotiation before you make a final decision. Once you make the decision to team, who you pick and why are just as important as who you exclude (accidentally or on purpose).

If you select to use a team, make sure you have pre-defined the negotiation strategy, have had the strategy signed-off by your boss or, for example, the company chief financial officer, if needed, and then run as many role-play sessions with the team as possible.

The team doesn't need to be physically present to play a role. They could be involved in sending emails to the other negotiating party, joining a conference call, or stepping into a meeting for a few minutes to deliver a specific message.

TACTIC #3: LACK OF AUTHORITY

When this tactic is used it is difficult to tell if the other person is telling the truth or telling a small lie. Have you ever had a salesperson say, "I need to check that with my boss, as I don't have the authority to approve that level of discount"? If yes, then it's very possible that you have had this tactic used on you in the past. Some negotiators will go to extreme lengths to make the tactic seem real, such as faking a phone call to their boss or leaving the room to get approval when all they are doing is making you wait while they check emails or play a quick video game. What this tactic does is set limits on the other negotiating party's concessions and makes it seem more difficult than it really is for you to reach a certain goal.

This tactic also guides you on what is and isn't possible. If the other negotiating party says they don't have authority, then they aren't necessarily saying no. It does highlight, however, that you are getting towards the higher or lower end/limit of their negotiation strategy. To call their bluff, in certain corporate settings, it is more than reasonable to end the negotiation and ask that their boss be included in the next session to stop wasting your time. This only really works if you are in a strong enough position to make that demand, though.

TACTIC #4: POLAR OPPOSITE

This tactic is often a good ploy to use when a negotiation is going in the wrong direction. As I am sure many people have experienced in the past, some negotiators can get unnecessarily confident, above and beyond the strength of their leverage or position. The Polar Opposite tactic allows you to reset their understanding of the negotiation boundaries and re-emphasize your power.

This tactic can be deployed by expressing the extreme opposite to the deal currently on the table. One example would be to threaten to end the negotiation or walk away. You can use phrases such as, "If we cannot reach an agreement on this particular contract term, then I will have no choice but to stop this meeting/discussion and go with the other provider." While a powerful tactic, if used too frequently or at the wrong time it can cause irritation and/or undermine the relationship you have built to date.

This tactic always reminds me of my father when I was growing up in Oxford, England. My father has always been a very calm and composed man. He would rarely ever raise his voice at my sister and I when we were kids, but when he did, we knew he was serious, and we were in trouble!

TACTIC #5: PLAN B

As boxer Mike Tyson once famously said, "Everyone has a plan until they get punched in the mouth."

You can have all the leverage in the world, from money to information, from competitive positioning to strategic relationships, but they mean very little if you have no other option but to sign a deal with one specific company or person.

One example we commonly see with startups is a lack of experience, resulting in lower leverage. Potential clients, who are often aware that startups need their business in order to survive, will take advantage of that fact. As a result of being in this position, companies will push for stricter terms or place emphasis on the risk of working with a much younger company in order to get a better deal.

Having an alternative option, a Plan B, only really works if that option is truly viable. Even if the other negotiating party is unaware that your alternative option is fake, it can still cause problems: impacting your team's confidence, stress, the speed and size of your concessions, and all the other hacks in this book.

In situations where you don't have a viable Plan B, the guidance is simple: work hard with as much time as you have available and get one.

TACTIC #6: TIME PRESSURE

In Chris Voss's book *Never Split The Difference*, a thrilling insight into the world of law enforcement negotiations, Chris highlights that "Time is one of the most crucial variables in any negotiation."[32] Time can be used to influence perceived scarcity, to create enough pressure to achieve additional concessions, and to change how a negotiation might end.

One application of this tactic is when a negotiation agenda is altered because the other negotiating party becomes aware of, for example, your departing flight heading home. If the other negotiating party believes you are under pressure to finish a negotiation by a specific time or to hit a certain target, such as an end-of-month sales quota, then you can almost certainly guarantee they will use that knowledge to their advantage.

To resolve this issue in a negotiation, challenge any deadlines you have been given, and if a deadline cannot be moved, try to avoid the other negotiating party being aware of your constraint.

TACTIC #7: STANDARDS

Another critical author and legend in the negotiations space is Stuart Diamond, CEO of Getting More Inc. and professor at the Wharton Business School, University of Pennsylvania. One of Diamond's impactful lessons is on the application of standards. This tactic is a negotiator's tool for referencing facts in order to justify a specific request or concession.[33] Standards are seen in a company's market positioning, brand, or even its publicly advertised value proposition. An example could be a manufacturing firm that advertises having 100% customer satisfaction guaranteed. If you experience anything less, you are more than justified in constantly referencing their customer satisfaction promise/statement the next time you meet them at the negotiation table. If a company does not deliver on their company promises, this significantly weakens their credibility (See "Ethos" back in chapter 2).

TACTIC #8: CONCESSIONS

Finally, let's discuss the importance of how to concede. Three rules should be applied to concede like a pro:

1. Never concede without getting something, however small, in return. This sets the tone for how you operate as a negotiator and will increase the value you extract from the other negotiating party;

2. If you have a list of concessions, structure the negotiation so that if you need to concede, you can proceed with the smaller ones first;

3. Have some sugar-coated concessions in your back pocket. These are concessions that hold greater tangible value for the other negotiating party than they cost you to provide. Examples could be free training or a longer contract term.

HACK ⑥ SUMMARY

a. Being prepared for a negotiation is critical. The more you prepare, the better the overall outcome.

b. While there is a seemingly endless (50+) list of tactics, there are eight that I believe everyone should know:

  i. <u>Set a strategy & anchor</u>: Ensure you understand the upper and lower limits of what you can and are willing to give up during a negotiation in order to get what you want. Align on these with your team or organization in advance, if needed, and clearly communicate your boundaries early on by anchoring.

  ii. <u>Teaming:</u> Use a team to help deliver your negotiation messaging, if and only if it adds value. Be aware of the fact that misalignment with your team can weaken your negotiation position.

  iii. <u>Lack of Authority</u>: If the other negotiation party expresses that they lack the authority to agree to a certain term or request, then be mindful they may be using this tactic to reduce their concessions. If appropriate, ask for the decision maker to join the next conversation.

iv. Polar Opposite: If you have reached a deadlock during a negotiation or find the other party is trying to take advantage of you and does not appreciate your position, don't hesitate to remind them of the fact that you can and will walk away.

v. Plan B: Always have a back-up plan if you can't reach the minimums you have set in your negotiation strategy. If you don't have a Plan B, get one.

vi. Time Pressure: Do not fall victim to time constraints unless you have no other choice.

vii. Standards: Refer to specific standards or known facts in order to ground the other negotiating party.

viii. Concessions: Only concede when you get something in return; concede small at first; have some concessions that are more meaningful to the other negotiating party than they are for you.

WHITE SPACE FOR NOTES

WHITE SPACE FOR NOTES

CONCLUSION

These six hacks are far from a complete list. However, I see them as the most critical ones to long term-negotiation karma. What I mean by that is that there are several other cheap tricks that may help you win a one-off negotiation but will ultimately have a detrimental effect if you ever need to deal with that individual or company or someone else in their close network ever again. Such tricks include but are not limited to lying, deception, misdirection, inconsistency, and coercion.

One additional element that is interwoven within many of these hacks is cultural influencing factors. I left this topic out on purpose, as it truly justifies an entire book of its own. The term "culture" is a complex consideration, arguably different for every single person. Culture also changes throughout your life based on your upbringing, experiences, and the people you engage with (such as family members, school friends, work colleagues, and mentors). While there are definitely some insightful generalizations that can be applied to understanding how to best interact with another person who was either born in or currently resides in a specific country and/or speaks a certain language, you can easily get lost by focusing on these guidelines in a vacuum. Two people and their research that I hold in high regard on this topic is Professor Gerard Hendrik Hofstede, a Dutch social psychologist and professor emeritus of Organizational Anthropology and International Management at Maastricht University in the Netherlands and Professor Wilhelmina Wosinska, Senior Lecturer in Social Psychology at Arizona State University. Professor Hofstede's main research website is a useful tool and is constantly updated with additional research insights: https://www.hofstede-insights.com. I recommend reading some of his research specific to a culture that you either communicate with on a regular basis or are about to start negotiating with to avoid any common mistakes. At the same time, it is also important to stay true to the core negotiation hacks in this book, as they generally apply across most cultural matrices with only a few exceptions.

What I love about this topic is that even though some of these key concepts can be traced back over two thousand years, psychologists and behavioral scientists are continuing to make new and relevant findings all the time. One of the most recent, at the time of this writing, was published by Dr. Orly Idan and Dr. Michael Reifen-Tagar in the *Journal of Psychological Science.* Dr. Idan and Dr. Reifen-Tagar argue that phrasing select communications in noun form instead of the verb form can reduce anger during a negotiation and improve the likelihood of a successful outcome.[34] An example could be the use of nouns in a sentence to say, "I am in support of the tightening of our service level agreements," rather than the same sentiment but in a verb-based sentence such as, "I am in support of tightening our service level agreements." This will have profound implications for how negotiation scripts can and should be written as part of your advance preparation . . . Hack #7?

ACKNOWLEDGMENTS

There are so many people who have contributed to this book for whom I am grateful beyond words. I would like to give thanks to the following people in particular:

My parents and my sister for their relentless support and for reading and giving their honest feedback on early drafts of the book;

To Clint Greenleaf for supporting my vision and mentoring me along with his team of world-class book publishing and production experts (notably, Kimberly Lance and Thom Lemmons);

To Dr. Ted Smith, whose linguistic expertise provided some critical guidance on how to best structure this book with the extensive audience in mind;

To Ari Ojalvo and George Fallica for their real time coaching on entrepreneurship and deal making;

To Brooke Bains for her partnership in the "Hacks Capital" journey and book edit suggestions;

To Guy Hubball for being an inspiring leader and supporting the publication of this book;

To Heather Dougherty for her literary comments on an early draft of the book and the idea to have a "White Space for Notes" section after each chapter;

To my wife, who gave me the space and coaching to ensure I finished the book and didn't procrastinate any longer.

NOTES/REFERENCES/CITATIONS

1. "Peter Drucker: Father of Modern Management", interview by Bill Moyers (November 17, 1988). New York, NY: Public Square Media.

2. Darwin, Charles. (1872). *The Expression of the Emotions in Man and Animals.* London: John Murray.

3. Chartrand, T. L., & Bargh, J. A. (1999). The Chameleon Effect: The Perception–Behavior Link and Social Interaction. *Journal of Personality and Social Psychology,* 76(6), 893–910.

4. Hall, Edward T. (1966). *The Hidden Dimension.* Garden City, NY: Anchor Books.

5. Mehrabian, Albert. (1981). *Silent Messages: Implicit Communication of Emotions and Attitudes.* University of Virginia, VA: Wadsworth Publishing Company (Cengage).

6. Jessen, Sarah and Tobias Grossman. (2014). "Unconscious Discrimination of Social Cues from Eye Whites in Infants." *Proceedings of the National Academy of Sciences of the United States of America* 111: 16208–16213

7. Binetti, N., Harrison, C., Coutrot, A., Johnston, A., and Mareschal, I. (2016). Pupil Dilation as an Index of Preferred Mutual Gaze Duration. *Royal Society Open Science,* 3(7), 160086

8. Miller, N., Maruyama, G., Beaber, R.J., and Valone, K. (1976). Speed of Speech and Persuasion. *Journal of Personality and Social Psychology*, 34, 615–624; Packwood, W.T. Loudness as a Variable in Persuasion. *Journal of Counseling Psychology*, 1974, 21, 1–2.

9. Huffington, Arianna. (2015). *Thrive: The Third Metric to Redefining Success and Creating a Life of Well-Being, Wisdom, and Wonder.* New York, NY: Crown Publishing Group.

10. Prince, Paul, Dan the Automator, Murphy, Róisín., and J-Live. (1999). "The Truth." New York, NY: Warner Music Group and Tommy Boy Records

11. Kennedy, George A. (1991). *Aristotle "On Rhetoric": A Theory of Civic Discourse.* New York/Oxford: Oxford University Press.

12. Zak, Paul J. (2017). *Trust Factor: The Science of Creating High-Performance Companies.* New York, NY: AMACOM.

13. Cooney, G., Gilbert, D. T., and Wilson, T. D. (2017). The Novelty Penalty: Why Do People Like Talking about New Experiences but Hearing about Old Ones? *Psychological Science*, 28, 380–394.

14. McCroskey, J. C. (1969). A Summary of Experimental Research on the Effects of Evidence in Persuasive Communication. *The Quarterly Journal of Speech*, 55, 169–176.

15. Rousseau, Jean-Jacques., Coleman, Patrick (Editor)., and Scholar, Angela (Translator). (2000). *Confessions* (Original Title: *Les Confessions*). Oxford, England. Oxford University Press (first published 1789).

16. Merenda, P. F. (1987). Toward a Four-Factor Theory of Temperament and/or Personality. *Journal of Personality Assessment.* 51: 367–374.

17. Clark, L. A., and Watson, D. (2008). Temperament: An Organizing Paradigm for Trait Psychology. In O. P. John, R. W. Robins, and L. A. Pervin (Eds.), *Handbook of Personality: Theory and Research* (3rd ed., pp.265–286). New York: Guilford Press.

18. Jung, Carl Gustav and Marie-Luise von Franz. (1964). *Man and His Symbols.* New York: Doubleday.

19. Marston, William M. (1999). *Emotions of Normal People.* Abingdon, Oxon: Routledge.

20. Keirsey, David and Bates, Marilyn (1984). *Please Understand Me: Character and Temperament Types.* Green Valley Lake, CA: Prometheus Nemesis Book Company.

21. Myers, I. and McCaulley, M. (1985) *Manual: A Guide to the Development and Use of the Myers-Briggs Type Indicator.* Mountain View, CA: Consulting Psychologists Press.

22. Kolb, D. A., and Fry, R. E. (1974). *Toward an Applied Theory of Experiential Learning.* Cambridge, MA: M.I.T. Alfred P. Sloan School of Management.

23. Ziglar, Zig. (1985). *Zig Ziglar's Secrets of Closing the Sale.* New York: Berkley.

24. Cialdini, Robert. (2006). *Influence: The Psychology of Persuasion.* New York: HarperBusiness.

25. Carnegie, Dale. (1998). *How to Win Friends and Influence People.* New York: Gallery.

26. Tamir, D. I. and Mitchell, J. P. (2012). Disclosing Information about the Self is Intrinsically Rewarding. *Proceedings of the National Academy of Sciences,* 109(21), 8038–8043

27. Sanders, Tim. (2005). *The Likeability Factor.* New York: Penguin Random House.

28. Hatfield, E., Cacioppo, J., and Rapson, R. L. (1994). *Emotional Contagion.* New York: Cambridge University Press.

29. Grant, Adam M., PhD. (2014). *Give and Take: A Revolutionary Approach to Success.* New York: Penguin Random House.

30. Aronson, E., Willerman, B., and Floyd, J. (1966). The Effect of a Pratfall on Increasing Interpersonal Attractiveness. *Psychonomic Science,* 4(6), 227–228

31. Giles, L. (2013). Sun Tzu *On The Art Of War.* Abingdon, Oxon: Routledge.

32. Voss, Chris and Raz, Tahl. (2016). *Never Split the Difference: Negotiating as if Your Life Depended on It.* New York: HarperBusiness.

33. Diamond, Stuart. (2012). *Getting More: How You Can Negotiate to Succeed in Work and Life.* New York: Crown Publishing Group.

34. Idan, O., Halperin, E., Hameiri, B., and Tagar, M. R. (2018). A Rose by Any Other Name? A Subtle Linguistic Cue Impacts Anger and Corresponding Policy Support in Intractable Conflict. *Psychological Science.* Volume: 29 issue: 6, page(s): 972–983.

ABOUT THE AUTHOR

Simon Rycraft is a profit and operations improvement expert/advisor who works with startups, private equity firms and the Fortune 500. Simon specializes in profit improvement, negotiation strategy development, coaching and training and has worked with companies across North America, Europe, Russia, India and South East Asia.

Simon holds a BA (Hons) in Business and Economics from the University of Nottingham, an MCIPS from the Chartered Institute of Procurement and Supply and an MBA from the Wharton Business School of the University of Pennsylvania.

www.ingramcontent.com/pod-product-compliance
Lightning Source LLC
Chambersburg PA
CBHW020547220526
45463CB00006B/2221